101 Coolest Things to Do

© 2017 101 Coolest Things

All rights reserved. No part of this publication may be reproduced, distributed, or transmitted in any form or by any means, including photocopying, recording, or other electronic or mechanical methods, without the prior written permission of the publisher, except in the case of brief quotations embodied in critical reviews and certain other noncommercial uses permitted by copyright law.

Introduction

So you're going to The Big Apple, huh? You lucky lucky thing! You are sure in for a treat because New York City is truly one of the most phenomenal cities on this planet.

This guide will take you on a journey through Manhattan, Brooklyn, Queens, the Bronx, and Staten Island to bring you the very best of this much loved city.

In this guide, we'll be giving you the low down on:
- the very best things to shove in your pie hole, from incredible sweet treats like Cronuts and Crack, through to the best places to get classic New York pizza
- incredible festivals, whether you would like to party to live bands, or you'd prefer to savour some New York wines at Brooklyn uncorked
- the coolest historical and cultural sights that you simply cannot afford to miss like the cities incredible

contemporary art museums, and some of the city's oldest churches

- the most incredible outdoor adventures, whether you fancy learning how to sail in a New York Park, or you fancy joining the youngsters of New York at an urban skate park
- the best spots for buying a New York souvenir, from scavenging through the city's labyrinthine flea markets to picking select items at upmarket boutiques
- the places where you can party like a local and make new friends
- and tonnes more coolness besides!

Let's not waste any more time – here are the 101 coolest things not to miss in New York City!

1. Indulge a Sweet Tooth With Some Crack Pie

And what on earth is crack pie, you ask? It's only the most addictive dessert on the planet, hence the name. This is a specialty of Momofuku Milk Bar, which you can find over in trendy Williamsburg, and it isn't the best thing to eat if you're watching your sugar intake, but for a decadent treat like no other it just cannot be beaten. The gooey filling in the centre of the pie is basically butter, milk, and eggs, but it's so much more than the sum of its parts. You'll be a convert from the first bite.

(382 Metropolitan Ave, Brooklyn; http://milkbarstore.com)

2. Have an Artsy Day at the MoMA

New York is one of the arts capitals of the universe, and in fact, it would be totally possible to spend an entire vacation trawling from gallery to gallery and ogling at the iconic works on display. But if you have limited time and can only fit a few galleries into your schedule, there's no question that the Museum of Modern Art needs to be one of them. Inside, you'll find incredible works of art from artists like

Frida Kahlo, Henri Matisse, Roy Lichtenstein, Andy Warhol, and many others besides.

(11 W 53rd St; www.moma.org)

3. Feel Magical at Tannen's Magic Store

There is a certain magic in the air on the streets of New York City, but there is one place where that sense of magic is amped up to the next level, and that's Tannen's Magic Store. Founded by Louis Tannen way back in 1925, this is the oldest operating magic store in the city, where you will be mesmerised by all kinds of quirky items, such as invisible paint, multiplying billiard balls, and rabbit producing top hats.

(45 W 34th St #608; www.tannens.com)

4. Have a True NYC Party Experience at 169 Bar

New York City is a place that offers many different things to many different people. It's an awesome place to eat for foodies, a treasure trove of galleries

for arts lovers, and for party-goers it offers the best all-nighters in the world. If you love nothing more than to party til dawn, we'd love to recommend a true New York style hotspot, 169 Bar. With palm trees, a leopard print pool table, and oysters and borscht on the menu, this place is out there in the best of ways, and a great place to dance and make new friends while you're in the city.
(169E Broadway; www.169barnyc.com)

5. Top Up Your Tan on Rockaway Beach

New York City is very unlikely to be one of the places that pops into your head when you think of stellar beach destinations. Okay, California and Hawaii and much more famous for their beautiful beaches, but let's not forget that New York is surrounded by water, and that means it's certainly not difficult to find a beach. Rockaway Beach can be found on the south shore of Long Island, and the beach is wide and clean. What more could you ask for on an NY summer day?

6. Line Up For a Morning Cronut

To say that New York is a foodie city is a massive understatement. There is the pizza, the bagels, the incredible Asian food, and lots more besides. And the latest bite to become popular in New York City is the cronut, something that you can only purchase from the Dominique Ansel Bakery in the Soho area. Every morning, there is a queue around the block for these croissant-doughnut hybrids, so be sure to get there as early as you can.

(189 Spring St; http://dominiqueansel.com)

7. Watch a Concert at the Iconic Carnegie Hall

There are so many performance spaces and cultural centres across New York City, but few have the iconic status that Carnegie Hall can claim to have. This concert hall, which can be found in midtown Manhattan, was created by the philanthropist Andrew Carnegie in 1891, and since then it has established itself as one of the most prestigious venues for classical and popular music concerts in the world. Since opening, artists as diverse as Judy Garland, The Beatles, and Tchaikovsky have taken to the stage.

(881 7th Avenue; www.carnegiehall.org)

8. Stroll the Oldest Bridge in NY, High Bridge

New York is a City that's surrounded by water, and this means that it's also a city where you can find many bridges. Only one of these can claim to be the oldest bridge in the city, and that would be High Bridge, which connects Manhattan and the Bronx. Unlike other bridges around the city, this particular bridge is only open to pedestrians and cyclists, so it's a great place to get some exercise, some peace, and incredible views.

(Harlem River Dr; www.nycgovparks.org/park-features/highbridge-park/planyc)

9. Check Out the Graffiti Art of Freedom Tunnel

New York is an arts city through and through, but you will get a very limited perspective of the city's creativity if you stick to the well known museums and galleries. It can also be a great idea to hit the streets, and you can find some incredible graffiti art in an abandoned tunnel called the Freedom Tunnel. Chris Pape, a highly respected graffiti artist, started creating his public artworks here in 1974, and it's still going strong today.

10. Fill Your Stomach With Grilled Mexican Corn From Café Habana

While you're in New York, you'll want to fill your stomach with local noms like pizza and bagels, but one of the great things about a cosmopolitan city like New York, is that you can find great food from all over. Great Mexican food is not difficult to find, but if there's one place that you can't miss it's Café Habana, which as you might have guessed from the name, also serves up Cuban dishes. Go for the grilled Mexican corn, smothered in cheese, mayo, and lime, and you'll be transported to Latin food heaven.

(17 Prince Street; www.cafehabana.com)

11. Say Hi to the Animals at Bronx Zoo

If you're an animal lover visiting New York City, a visit to the Bronx Zoo, which happens to be the largest metropolitan zoo in the United States, needs to be at the very top of your list. Spread across 265 acres of land, there is so much to explore, and you are sure to be entertained during your trip whether adult or child. You'll get to discover Tiger Mountain, the World of Reptiles, the Big Bears, and more besides.

(2300 Southern Blvd, Bronx; www.bronxzoo.com)

12. Take in a Baseball Game at the Yankee Stadium

Americans love baseball, and if you are a sports lover, there is little that would be more exciting than actually seeing a live baseball game in person while

you're in the country. Fortunately for you, New York is home to one of the most famous baseball teams on the planet, the New York Yankees. The home of the Yankees is, of course, the famous Yankee Stadium, which can be found in the Bronx. The stadium can be filled with 50,000 people, so it's a guarantee that the atmosphere will be electric.
(1 E 161st St, Bronx;
http://newyork.yankees.mlb.com/nyy/ballpark/index.jsp)

13. Indulge With Maple Bacon Cookies From Shmackary's

If you travelled all the way to New York City just to eat delicious things, you could spend a year there and still have more treats to discover. This means you'll need to prioritise what you put into your gob, and the maple bacon cookies at Shmackary's are a must try. Maple and bacon are a well worn combination with pancakes, but this is the only place where we've seen the combo in cookie form. And once you're done with those, this cookie joint has 45 other flavours to choose from.

(362 W 45th St; http://schmackarys.com)

14. Take a Ride on the Coney Island Cyclone

Coney Island exists in the lower part of Brooklyn, and it is most famous for its amusement park and boardwalk attractions. There are countless ways to stay entertained at Coney Island, and taking a ride on the famous Coney Island Cyclone might just be the most fun experience of all. This wooden rollercoaster opened all the way back in 1927, and it's still possible for thrill seekers to take a ride today.

(1000 Surf Ave; http://lunaparknyc.com)

15. Learn Something New at the New York Transit Museum

Since New York is such a cultural city with so many museums, you might not think that a museum dedicated to the city's public transit would be all that interesting, but the New York Transit Museum in so well put together that it's definitely worth a visit on a grey morning. What's more, the museum is located in an actual subway station, where you get to learn about the Subway system, public buses, and other railway lines.

(99 Schermerhorn St, Brooklyn; www.nytransitmuseum.org)

16. Feel the Ker-Ching of Cash on Wall Street

Wall Street is a part of New York City that is known, for better or for worse, all around the world. It is the heartland of America's capitalism and the heart of New York's business district, where financial professionals toil 24 hours a day. Although you won't be able to go into all the buildings, Wall Street is somewhere to visit if you want a slice of iconic NYC. There are also some walking tours that will give you a more comprehensive history of the area.

17. Eat at a Historic Restaurant, Delmonico's

In New York City, it's not difficult to find a great eatery on virtually every single one of the city streets, but there's only a handful that can claim to be historic New York institutions, and Delmonico's is certainly one of those. This restaurant first opened all the way back in 1827, and it's claimed that this is the first restaurant in the city to allow diners to order a la carte. These days, they are still serving up incredible steaks and other classics, but be sure to book a table in advance.

(56 Beaver Street; www.delmonicosrestaurant.com)

18. Take a Horse and Carriage Ride in Central Park

We know that it's a total cliché, but we think that taking a horse and carriage ride in Central Park might be so cheesy that it has looped back round to being cool again. And truthfully, in the time we live in, when speed is valued so highly, this is a great way to actually slow down and enjoy the journey itself. It's super touristy, but it's kind of okay to do touristy things when you are actually a tourist, right?

19. Feel the Stretch of History at Trinity Church on Broadway

When you think of world cities well known for their religious architecture, European cities like Rome and London are likely to spring to mind. But if you keep your eyes open, you'll also find some stunning religious buildings in New York. Our favourite of these might just be Trinity Church, which is located on Broadway. The church has 300 years of history, but the building as it's seen today dates to the mid 19th century. For a little respite from honking horns and hot dog vendors, the church is an oasis of calm. *(75 Broadway; www.trinitywallstreet.org)*

20. Be Awed by the New York by Gehry Building

Even if you aren't somebody who is into architecture, chances are that you have heard of Frank Gehry and his buildings that have made him an iconic figure in the design world. If you fancy checking out one of his buildings in person, New York by Gehry, otherwise known as 8 Spruce Street, is the place to be. This is the tallest residential building in all of the Americas, containing 898 highly sought after rental units.

(http://newyorkbygehry.com)

21. Gorge on Dumplings at Prosperity Dumpling

If you want Asian food, take a trip to Asia, right? Right. Well, Asia or New York. Because frankly it's easier to find all kinds of Asian food in New York than it is in virtually any other place in the world. But you have to pay through the nose for New York style Asian grub, right? In some places, but not if you head to Prosperity Dumpling where you can gorge on dumplings and scallion pancakes for just a few dollars.

(2369 86th St, Brooklyn)

22. Get Geeky at MoMath, the Museum of Mathematics

New York is extremely well known for its breadth of incredible galleries and art spaces, but if you are more likely to geek out over maths and science, you aren't left behind with a visit to the Museum of Mathematics. A fairly recent addition to the NY scene since it only opened in 2012, this museum is dedicated to enhancing public understanding and perception of mathematics, with interactive exhibits and lots of fun events.

(11 E 26th St; http://momath.org)

23. Savour the Old School Luxury of Bergdorf Goodman

If your favourite free-time activity is to shop until you drop, you have certainly made it to the right city. New York is the kind of place where you can find grungy flea markets and luxury stores alike, and on the luxurious side of thing it doesn't get better than Bergdorf Goodman, a luxury goods store that opened in 1928 on Fifth Avenue. Inside, you'll find boutiques from the likes of Chanel, Gucci, Versace and Yves Saint Laurent.

(754 Fifth Avenue; www.bergdorfgoodman.com)

24. Transport Yourself to Another World at Belvedere Castle

The image that most people have of New York is a place with tall buildings, incredible shopping, and restaurants that are open 24 hours. While all this is true, it doesn't tell the complete story of the city, and to get a different perspective, a trip to Belvedere Castle in Central Park is a must. This ornamental building was built as a Victorian folly in 1869, serving no other purpose than to be grand and beautiful. It provides incredible views across the park and the city.

(www.centralparknyc.org/things-to-see-and-do/attractions/belvedere-castle.html)

25. Get Decadent at the Grand Central Oyster Bar

Grand Central Station is one of the most important transport hubs in all of the United States, but even if you don't need to go there to catch a train, it's well worth checking the place out for its sense of history, and for the incredible Grand Central Oyster Bar, which you'll find on the lower level of the building. This oyster bar has a history dating all the way back to 1913, and it's still one of the best places in the city to eat oysters and other fresh seafood. Why not get a little decadent, huh?

(www.oysterbarny.com)

26. Get Literary at the Edgar Allen Poe Cottage

Edgar Allen Poe might just be the most famous horror writer in literary history, and if you are a fan of the man and his works, it's well worth taking a trip into the Bronx where you can visit Edgar Allen Poe Cottage, the former home of the man himself. The house has been restored to its original appearance so you can see it just as it was when Poe lived there, and taking a guided tour is a great idea to have the full experience.

(2640 Grand Concourse, Bronx;
http://bronxhistoricalsociety.org/poe-cottage)

27. Learn About NY's Immigrant History at the Tenement Museum

The United States is a nation that has welcomed immigrants for hundreds of years, and New York on the East Coast is one place that has a particularly strong history of welcoming history into its fold. From 1863 to 1935, a tenement building on the lower east side played host to an estimated 7000 people from twenty different nations, and today that building is dedicated to documenting the immigrant experience in New York, depicting the lives of the families who lived in this particular building.
(103 Orchard Street; http://tenement.org)

28. Take a Ceramics Class at La Mano Pottery

If you think of yourself as a creative kind of person, New York is a city that will embrace you wholeheartedly because New York is also a deeply creative place, and it offers many opportunities for creative types to get their artistic juices flowing. One place to get creative and have a whole lot of fun is at La Mano Pottery, a ceramics studio with a full range of classes for kids, adults, total beginners, and more experienced potters alike.

(110 W 26th St; www.lamanopottery.com)

29. Down Cocktails on the Met's Roof Garden

Thanks to popular shows like Sex and the City, the idea of drinking cocktails is totally intertwined with NYC. As a result, there's no shortage of places to get a great cocktail and a great view at the same time, and one of the loveliest of these places is the roof garden of the Metropolitan Museum of Art. Throughout the week, this rooftop is a café, and on Friday and Saturday nights it becomes a Martini bar with decadent drinks and spectacular views.

(1000 5th Avenue; www.metmuseum.org/visit/met-fifth-avenue)

30. Visit the Tiniest Museum in the City, Mmuseumm

New York City is a veritable haven for museum lovers, but there is of course only one museum that can claim to be the smallest of all the museums in the city, and that's Mmuseumm in lower Manhattan, a space that is dedicated to the overlooked, dismissed, or ignored. And in this city of bright lights, Mmuseumm's focus on the little things is a refreshing change. This teeny tiny place only fits three people at a time, so it's probably best for a solo visit.

(4 Cortlandt Alley; www.mmuseumm.com)

31. Take in the Views From the Deck of the Staten Island Ferry

Staten Island is very much the forgotten borough of New York City, even though it has a population of around half a million people, and it's well worth a visit, not least because that gives you an excuse to ride the Staten Island Ferry, which is a legitimate part of local history. The ferry began operation in 1817, long before locals drove around or took the subway, and the 5 mile ride is totally free. There are also wonderful views from the deck.

(www.siferry.com)

32. Take in a Concert at the Brooklyn Academy of Music

New York is a cultural city through and through, and you will be able to catch hundreds of different kinds of performances on any night of the week, and if you want to know the place to catch the best contemporary and avant-garde performances, the Brooklyn Academy of Music would be a very good place to start. It's also good to know that there are often free performances in the centre's café, so keep up with their schedule of events if you're on a budget.

(30 Lafayette Avenue, www.bam.org)

33. Watch a Cult Classic Movie at Syndicated Cinema

You could spend a whole year in New York, and still have more museums to visit, more parks to stroll, and more restaurants to eat at. But sometimes all you really want to do is take it easy and watch a great movie, right? When that moment strikes, you need to know about Syndicated Cinema. This cinema is a very recent addition to the Brooklyn scene, screening classic films from the past and recent independent films. There's also a restaurant and cocktail bar on-site.

(40 Bogart St, Brooklyn; http://syndicatedbk.com)

34. Go Ice Skating on Wollman Rink

New York is a city of extremes. The summers are blisteringly hot, and the winters are chill inducing to say the least. But even if you're not somebody who loves the cold, you can't help but be taken by New York City's festive spirit during those colder months. And what better way to enjoy the nip in the air than with a fun ice skating experience in the outdoors? Wollman Rink is an outdoor rink in Central Park that's been a destination for families, couples, and groups of friends since 1950, with a wonderful backdrop of NY buildings and the twinkling stars by night.

(830 5th Ave; www.wollmanskatingrink.com)

35. Sip on Cocktails at The Dead Rabbit Grocery and Grog

If you're into cocktails, you sure are in luck because there's a wealth of cocktail bars dotted around every nook and cranny of New York City, but for us, The Dead Rabbit Grocery and Grog, in spite of the weird name, is a cocktail joint that is extra special. We're particularly into the Fun Lovin' Criminal, which is a mix of tequila, rose vermouth, apple brandy, grapefruit, and hops. And if you want something a little more straight shooting, they also have a killer Irish whiskey menu.

(30 Water St, www.deadrabbitnyc.com)

36. Wave a Rainbow Flag at NYC Pride

NYC is one of the most diverse cities in the world, in a whole range of ways, and it's an incredible place to be an LGBT person in the 21st century. Of course, it wasn't always that way, but NYC has always been at the forefront of the gay rights movement, and attending NYC Pride is a great way to celebrate all the achievements of the city, and all the incredible colours of this community. Pride takes place in June each year, so why not show up and join in with all the fun?

(www.nycpride.org)

37. Party Hard at the Governors Ball

Although New York City is party central and you can find places to dance on any night of the week, it's not quite so established on the summer festival scene. But one New York festival that party lovers won't want to miss is the annual Governors Ball. Despite only launching in 2011, this summer festival has already gained iconic status with a great mix of different music. Previous acts that have taken to the stage include The Killers, M83, and Florence and the Machine. It's hosted on Randall's Island in June of each year.

(www.governorsballmusicfestival.com)

38. Enjoy a Classic Cheeseburger at Joe Jr

When you think of American food, what is the first thing that springs into your mind? A good old fashioned burger, right? A trip to New York wouldn't be complete without chowing down on at least one burger, and our favourite of all the New York burgers can be found at Joe Jr, an East Village classic that looks a little rough around the edges but serves up the best cheeseburger to be found, well, anywhere.

(167 3rd Avenue)

39. Feel NY's Creativity at the FIT Museum

As you walk around the streets of New York, it quickly becomes apparent that this is a very stylish city indeed, but in spite of this there is only one museum dedicated to fashion in the whole city and that's the Museum at the Fashion Institute of Technology. As well as showcasing incredible couture garments, and artefacts pertaining to the fashion world, there's also a great programme of events, including talks with leading designers, workshops, and book signings.

(227 W 27th St; www.fitnyc.edu/museum)

40. Check Out Nathan's Hot Dog Eating Contest

If you're visiting New York from outside of the United States, you are likely to be a little surprised by the portion sizes that you'll experience while you are in the city. Yep, Americans like to eat, and this is never more evident than at the annual Nathan's Hot Dog Eating Contest. The contest take place on Coney Island every July 4th, and it has a history that dates all the way back to 1916. The most hot dogs anyone has managed to eat in a 10 minute period is seventy. Woah.

(www.nathansfamous.com/hot-dog-eating-contest)

41. Keep Kids Happy at the Brooklyn Children's Museum

Travelling with kids can be a pleasure, but it's also a lot of hard work. And so when in New York City, a trip to the Brooklyn Children's Museum is an absolute must. This was the first museum in the country to specifically cater to children, and it's a place where they'll have fun and learn something new at the same time. All the exhibitions are really hands on, giving your kids the opportunity to learn about world cultures, history, science, the art world, and more.

(45 Brooklyn Ave, Brooklyn, www.brooklynkids.org)

42. Enjoy the Colours of Macy's Flower Show

Macy's is one of New York's most iconic department stores. It opened all the way back in the 1850s and has been delighting customers ever since then. There's no bad time to visit Macy's and indulge in some retail therapy, but we specially love the time of year when they put on their annual

Flower Show. Each March, the NY store is taken over with incredible blooms of flowers, transforming it into a nature lover's paradise.
(www.macys.com/social/flower-show)

43. Find Some Refuge at the New York Botanical Garden

If you have planned a trip to New York City, it's likely that you enjoy city life and can cope with metropolises, but even city people need a breather now and again, and that's when you make your way to the very beautiful New York Botanical Garden. Located in the Bronx, this 250 acre oasis contains more than one million living plants from tropical, temperate, and desert climates.
(2900 Southern Blvd, Bronx; www.nybg.org)

44. Tour the NY Distilling Company

There's definitely no shortage of places to enjoy a drink or two while you're in New York city, but there have been surprisingly few New York based

distilleries until recently. This is because it was only recently that distillery licenses were reduced from $50,000 to just over $1k. And one of the best new distilleries to emerge from this change is the NY Distilling Company in Williamsburg, Brooklyn. They specialise in gins with lots of botanicals, and they give free tours and tastings on the weekends.
(75 Richardson St, Brooklyn; www.nydistilling.com)

45. Catch a Matinee on Broadway

We know that watching a show on Broadway is kind of an obvious thing to do, but that doesn't mean that it's not super cool. In fact, we think that the theatre scene, particularly if you're into musical theatre, is like nowhere else in the world in wonderful New York. Because theatre tickets can be on the expensive side, we would recommend catching a matinee performance if you want to have some spare change for dinner.

46. Learn to Sail at Flushing Meadows Park

Of all the places in the world where you might think you could learn to sail, Queens in New York is probably not somewhere that would spring to mind. But lo and behold, the city that has it all can even help you out with this! This park doesn't even have a beach, but it does have a gigantic lake that is the setting for sailing lessons in the city. If you fancy trying your hand at something new and enjoying the city in a totally different way, why not give it a go? *(www.nycgovparks.org/parks/flushing-meadows-corona-park)*

47. Get a Bagel With Everything at Brooklyn Bagel

Bagels are one of those New York signature foods that you have to try while you're in the city. We know that they offer no nutritional value, that they probably do your body more harm than good – but they taste amazing! And for a bagel like no other, Brooklyn Bagel is the place to be. Whether you want a classic plain bagel with cream cheese, or you fancy pushing the boat out with onions, multi-seeds, cinnamon or anything else, this is the place to get your bagel hit.

(286 8th Ave #1; http://bkbagel.com)

48. Learn Something New at the American Museum of Natural History

New York City is probably more famous for its art museums than other types of museums, but actually it contains some of the greatest learning institutions to be found anywhere in the world. The American Museum of Natural History is one of the world's largest museums, and in our opinion, one of the greatest too. With around 33 million specimens of fossils, animals, plants, minerals, rocks, meteorites, human remains and more, there is plenty to explore.

(Central Park West & 79th St; www.amnh.org)

49. Enjoy Some Classic Cheesecake at Junior's in Brooklyn

New Yorkers sure do know how to indulge, and this is especially apparent when you tuck into a slice (or five) of classic New York cheesecake. For our money, the best place for a slice of the good stuff is at Junior's in Brooklyn. This is a classic Brooklyn diner that dates back to a time when Brooklyn wasn't hipster central in any way, shape or form. Similarly, the cheesecake is no frills, but that doesn't stop people travelling from all over the city to savour some of the yumminess.

(386 Flatbush Ave Ext, Brooklyn; www.juniorscheesecake.com)

50. Visit Manhattan's Oldest Church, St Paul's Chapel

New York City hasn't always been the bustling metropolis as we know it today, and taking a stroll in Lower Manhattan to St Paul's Chapel is a great way of getting a sense of the city in the centuries gone by. This church was built all the way back in 1766, making it the oldest church in the whole city, and at the time of being built it was also the city's tallest building, although these days it is eclipsed by the many NY skyscrapers. St Paul's is still an active church with services and weekday concerts.

(209 Broadway; www.trinitywallstreet.org/about/stpaulschapel)

51. Check Out the Sculptures of Isamu Noguchi at the Noguchi Museum

Queens is one of the boroughs of New York that all too often gets left out when thinking of cool days out, but there are so many cool things to do in Queens that we could have written a whole guide about this part of NY alone. One of the coolest spots definitely has to be the Noguchi Museum, an arts centre created by the Japanese-American sculptor, Isamu Noguchi. When you're in need of some tranquillity, the Sculpture Garden is a wonderful place to escape to on a bustling New York day (i.e. every day).

(9-01 33rd Rd, Queens; www.noguchi.org)

52. Rock Out at the Bowery Ballroom

New York is a city with a fabulous live music culture, and if indie bands are up your alley, we reckon that Bowery Ballroom is the best place to check them out in the city. The building was constructed just before the Wall Street Crash of the 1920s, but only became a music venue in the late 90s. This is very much the place where you would discover an up and coming band you haven't heard of while making friends with locals over a pint of beer, which doesn't sound at all bad to us.

(6 Delancey Street; www.boweryballroom.com)

53. Indulge a Carnivore at Keen's Steakhouse

A holiday to NYC is certainly not the time to be on a diet, and what better way to treat yourself on a trip to the Big Apple than with a juicy steak? For our money, the best place for a juicy slab of meat is Keen's Steakhouse, which has been pleasing its meat loving customers since 1885. Everything on the menu here is good, but it's the mutton chops that stand out.

(72 W 36th St; www.keens.com)

54. Catch a Movie at the Tribeca Film Festival

Some of the greatest movie directors, producers, and actors have emerged from the New York arts scene, and if you are somebody who loves going to the movies, tying in a New York trip with the Tribeca Film Festival is a fantastic idea. This is the place to steer clear of blockbuster films and see some of the coolest independent movies, documentaries, and shorts from up and coming names. It takes place in April each year.
(https://tribecafilm.com)

55. Escape City Life at Jamaica Bay Wildlife Refuge

The United States is a huge country with lots of open space and different landscapes, so it's unlikely that nature lovers would go out of their way to have an outdoor adventure in NYC. But with that said, there are definitely some hidden green gems for outdoorsy types, and we are particularly enamoured by the Jamaica Bay Wildlife Refuge. The water and salt marches lie between Brooklyn and Queens, with lots of dunes, brackish, ponds, and fields to be explored when you need a break from honking horns and neon lights.

(www.nyharborparks.org/visit/jaba.html)

56. Tour the House of a Jazz Music Legend

New York is a city that has been home to all kinds of legends of the film, art, and music world, and an iconic New Yorker name that everybody knows is Louis Armstrong. While you're in the city, it's possible to visit Louis Armstrong House, which was the home of the legend and his wife Lucille from 1943 to 1971. The house is now a tribute to the man's life and legacy, and it's still furnished as it was when he lived there.

(34-56 107th St, Flushing; http://louisarmstronghouse.org)

57. Sip on Great Beers at Gottscheer Hall

We know that there's no shortage of watering holes in New York, but if you are not the kind of person who wants fancy cocktails and you just want a great tasting glass of beer, we've got just the place for you: Gottscheer Hall. Located in Queens, this is an old fashioned German beer hall that was opened by immigrants in 1924. Once inside, you'll think that you're in Germany, and the imported German beers as well as the krainerwurst and spaetzli always go down a treat.

(657 Fairview Ave, Ridgewood; http://gottscheerhall.com)

58. Take in a View of Brooklyn From the Red Hook Warehouse

Red Hook Warehouse, otherwise known as The Liberty Warehouse, is a place that tourists don't often visit, and indeed, it's a place that many local people don't know about either. This forgotten storehouse dates back to 1913, and sits on the Brooklyn waterfront. Although it may not be that well known, it's the tallest building in Brooklyn by quite a way, and if you ascend to the rooftop, you can enjoy incredible views of the city around you.

(260 Conover St, Brooklyn; http://thelibertywarehouse.com)

59. Tuck Into a Slice From Koronet Pizza

New York and pizza slices are a hand and a glove, and a trip to the Big Apple without at least one slice of pizza would be criminal. To be honest, that's an unlikely story, but the question still lingers of where to find the best slice? There are so many places but in limiting ourselves to one pizza joint in this book, we're going for Koronet Pizza on Broadway, which sells jumbo slices that are bigger than a human head. You're welcome.

(2848 Broadway; www.koronetpizzany.com)

60. Go Mountain Biking in Wolfe's Pond Park

Believe it or not, there are more green spaces in New York City than Central Park. Yes, you might have to look to the outer boroughs, but if you're a green or an adventure lover, this is well worth the effort. Take the ferry over to Staten Island and you will find Wolfe's Pond Park, which is the kind of park that serves many different purposes. There's a beach on the south edge of the park, there's lovely marshland and nature, and for adventure lovers, there's a 4 mile bike trail that will satisfy a need for speed.

(420 Cornelia Ave, Staten Island; www.nycgovparks.org/parks/wolfes-pond-park)

61. Stock Up on Sweets at Economy Candy

If you are travelling with kids, or you just happen to be a big kid yourself, we know somewhere that might just send you giddy with joy, and that's Economy Candy. This might just be the most seriously sugary spot that we've ever seen. With a history that dates back to 1937, Economy Candy is an NYC institution, selling candies that are both vintage and modern. Just be sure to pace yourself with all of that sugar!

(108 Rivington Street; www.economycandy.com)

62. Watch an Outrageous Art Show at Gowanus Ballroom

A night out at the opera or at Carnegie Hall is never going to be a bad thing, but these kind of established venues only show one side of New York, and this has always been a city that has existed on the cutting edge. If you fancy catching a performance that is totally Avant Garde, Gowanus Ballroom will be more up your alley. This is an alternative arts space in Brooklyn that has garnered a reputation as a place where you can see outrageous shows from up and coming performance artists.
(55 9th Street, Brooklyn; http://gowanusballroom.com)

63. Indulge a Vintage Lover at Brooklyn Flea

As you walk along the streets of Brooklyn, you'll be in doubt that you have found yourself in Hipsterville where a lot of attention is paid to wearing awesome threads. If you'd like to take back a little bit of the Brooklyn vibe with you, a trip to the weekly Brooklyn Flea is definitely in order. You'll find a treasure trove of vintage clothing, but if that's not your thing, you'll also find antiques, collectables, and a huge street food area where you can chow down.

(1 Hanson Pl, Brooklyn; www.brooklynflea.com)

64. Have an Art Filled Day at the Guggenheim Museum

The Guggenheim is one of the best known art museums anywhere in the world. It opened all the way back in 1939 with Solomon R. Guggenheim's private collections, and since then has expanded to contain an incredible variety of Impressionist, Post-Impressionist, and contemporary art. With works from the likes of Paul Klee, Picasso, Chagall, and Miro, this is truly an art lover's paradise.

(1071 5th Ave; www.guggenheim.org)

65. Eat Latin American Grub at Red Hook Food Vendors

The Red Hook Food Vendors Marketplace is a Brooklyn institution, and it's where the Latin community of New York gathers to eat the really authentic dishes from Latin America. If it's good enough for Latino locals, it's certainly good enough

for us, and some of the delicious bites you might stumble upon include elotes, hulks of corn covered in mayo, cheese, lime and chilli, huaraches, massive tortillas slathered in meat and cheese, and plantain chips. The trucks are open on weekends between April and October.
(160 Bay Street; Brooklyn)

66. Play Arcade Games While Drinking at Barcade

New York is the kind of city that offers everybody the opportunity to find their tribe, and if you like the idea of sipping on some really high quality beers while playing video games, you're in luck, because Barcade, a cool bar in Brooklyn, offers just that and was made with people like you in mind. This microbrewery has a tonne of local beers on tap, there is not a Fosters in sight, and the walls are covered with back to back old arcade machines so that you can have fun while you enjoy delicious beers. For real, what could be better?
(388 Union Ave, Brooklyn; http://barcadenewyork.com)

67. Take a Ride on Deno's Wonder Wheel

On a sunny day in New York City, we always take the Subway down to Coney Island to enjoy the boardwalk and ride some of the rides. One of the rides that you won't miss on the Brooklyn skyline in Deno's Wonder Wheel, a 150 feet tall Ferris Wheel that opened way back in 1920. Since then, 35 million people have taken a ride on the wheel, enjoying the view from the top with family and friends. Will you make it 35 million and one?

(3059 Denos D. Vourderis Place, Brooklyn; www.wonderwheel.com)

68. Take a Street Art Tour of NYC

One of the things that makes New York such an incredibly alive city is its diversity and welcoming attitude towards all different kinds of people. This means that the arts culture of New York is not limited to grand works set behind glass in museums, and it extends out on to the streets as well. Brooklyn

is a particularly interesting area for street art because it was once pretty run down, and has since become a very trendy place, putting its artists into the spotlight. You can walk the streets of Williamsburg and check out the art, or join one of the guided tours to get a better idea of its history and culture.
(www.freetoursbyfoot.com/new-york-tours/brooklyn-tours/williamsburg-street-art-tour)

69. Shop Avant Garde Labels at Dover Street Market

As you walk the streets of New York City, you can't fail to recognise that New Yorkers sure are a stylish bunch. If you'd like to sample some of that gorgeous style for yourself, you need to know where to go, and Dover Street Market is one of our favourite places to bankrupt ourselves for the sake of fashion. This is where you'll find trendy boutiques, not the major designers nor the grungy vintage clothes. Just be warned, you might want to take a backup credit card.

(160 Lexington Avenue; www.doverstreetmarket.com)

70. Gorge on Sugar at Veniero's Pastry Shop

The United States is the land of excess, and let's face it, it's not a place where you are going to have a hard time indulging a sweet tooth. But not all of the places that serve up sweet treats are equal, and we think that you only deserve the best. That's why Veniero's Pastry Shop needs to become etched into your brain. This is a traditional Italian bakery that opened way back in 1894, and it's the Italian staples like cannolis, biscottis, and tiramisu that locals, whether Italian or not, keep coming back for.
(342 E 11th St; http://venierospastry.com)

71. Read a Book in Greenacre Park

When you think of green spaces in New York, your mind will probably wander to images of Central Park and horse and carriage rides, but actually there are many more green spaces in the city, and Greenacre Park is one of the hidden gems. This park covers only a 7th of an acre, but in that space

there is a waterfall, and a charming outdoor café. It's the perfect place to while away a Spring Sunday in New York with a great book.
(217 E 51st St)

72. Immerse Yourself in Nostalgia at the Museum of the American Gangster

If you can't get enough of movies like Goodfellas and Scarface, you'll be well acquainted with the idea of the American gangster. But while these are excellent stories, the world of the American gangster extends way beyond fiction, and a place where you can get to grips with this underworld is at the Museum of the American Gangster, which you can find in Manhattan's East Village. Located in a former speakeasy, it's particularly great for learning about crime and gangsters in the Prohibition era.
(80 St Marks Pl;
http://siteline2.vendini.com/site/museumoftheamericangangster.org)

73. Discover a World of Rum at Van Brunt Stillhouse

In the 19th century, Brooklyn was a major hub for distilleries producing whiskey, gin, and rum, but when the Prohibition era kicked in, all of that changed. Only recently have the distillery licenses dropped in price, which means there is a brand new culture of distilling alcohol in the New York borough. One of the most celebrated of these distilleries in Van Brunt Stillhouse, which is one of few that has a focus on making its own rum. Be sure to book in advance for a tour, but you can pop in at any time for a cocktail or two.

(6 Bay St, Brooklyn; www.vanbruntstillhouse.com)

74. Watch a Show at United Palace Theatre

Built in the 1930s, United Palace is one of the New York places that has steadily become an institution and an essential part of the city's cultural makeup. Part church, music venue, and part non-profit cultural centre, this is a place where something cool is happening on every day of the week, guaranteed.

And if you're into music, do keep up with their programme, because artists like Bob Dylan, The Smashing Pumpkins, and Sonic Youth have performed here.

(4140 Broadway; www.unitedpalace.org)

75. Have a Kayaking Adventure at Pier 26

Okay, New York City may not be the immediate choice of vacation destination if you like relaxing experiences in nature, but look hard enough and you'll even be able to find that in this magical city. Pier 26 is a recent addition to the peaceful Hudson River Park, and here you will find a boathouse that offers kayaking trips on the Hudson during the spring and summer months of the year at absolutely no cost. What's stopping you?

(Pier 26, Hudson River Park; www.downtownboathouse.org/pier26)

76. Watch Offbeat Films at Spectacle Theater

If you're a real cinema buff, you might want to forsake another trip to another museum for some time spent in a movie theatre watching a film. There are so many cool movie theatres to choose from in the city, but we really love Spectacle Theater in Brooklyn when we want to watch something away from the mainstream. Located in trendy Williamsburg, this theatre is committed to screening overlooked works and forgotten gems. Just remember to bring your own snacks because no food or drinks are sold on the premises.
(124 S 3rd Street, Brooklyn; www.spectacletheater.com)

77. Indulge at Steve's Authentic Key Lime Pies

Okay, key lime pie is not a New York dessert – it comes from the sunshine state of Florida. But it's still a wholesome piece of Americana, and with key lime pies as good as the ones found at Steve's Authentic Key Lime Pies in Brooklyn, we think that you'd be a fool not to indulge in at least one slice on your visit to the Big Apple. And if you fancy trying

out a new take on the key lime pie, you can eat a chocolate covered pie on a stick. Need we say more?
(185 Van Dyke St, Brooklyn; http://stevesauthentic.com/wpnew)

78. Ride at Pony at the Bronx Equestrian Center

Once you get out of the centre of New York City, you'll be surprised at how the height of the buildings shrink, and at how the green spaces start to open up. If you'd like to have some time in nature while you're in the city, and you're somebody who likes doing things rather than trawling museum aisles, a trip to the Bronx Equestrian Center is a great idea. They provide horse riding lessons for all abilities, and can take you on trails through the nearby Pelham Bay Park.
(9 Shore Road, Bronx; www.bronxequestriancenter.com)

79. Explore a French Gothic Treasure, Grace Church

For fans of architecture, New York is pretty much a dream city, and there's more to explore than high-rises and tenements. One of the most unique and special buildings in Manhattan is Grace Church, one of the earliest examples of Gothic architecture in the city, and it was designed by James Renwick, who was only 24 years old at the time of the church being built. Although it opened way back in 1867, the church still functions and has regular services today.

(802 Broadway; http://gracechurchnyc.org)

80. Tuck Into Killer Barbecue at John Brown Smokehouse

If you do nothing more than eat some really great food during your time in New York, we think that will be time very well spent. The only condition is that you have to visit John Brown Smokehouse in Long Island at least once. This is the place to be for an old fashioned Kansas City style barbecue. We don't know how to begin to describe this haven of meaty deliciousness. The ribs, the baked beans, the mac and cheese, the corn pudding! It's all incredible. *(10-43 44th Dr, Long Island City; www.johnbrownseriousbbq.com)*

81. Enjoy All the Fun of Clearwater Festival

While New York is a centre for great music and great parties, it's not as famous for hosting epic music festivals as the west coast. But if you are a festival lover, New York still has something very special to offer in the form of Clearwater Festival, which has been held at Croton Point Park on the Hudson River for three decades now. The mission of the festival is to raise environmental awareness while having a great time, and previous acts that have played include Ani DiFranco, Tom Paxton, and more. It's hosted in June each year.
(www.clearwaterfestival.org)

82. Ride an Insect Carousel in the Bronx

Bronx Zoo is definitely one of the major attractions not only of the Bronx but of all New York, and we think it's more than possible to spend consecutive days there and still have things to see. One of the quirkier things that you can find within the park is the Bug Carousel, a carousel that features 64 different types of insects that you can mount. It's designed to be both fun and educational for kids, and it makes for great souvenir photos.

(2300 Southern Blvd, Bronx; www.bronxzoo.com)

83. Do a Contemporary Art Crawl of Chelsea

New York City is an incredible arts destination, and the Chelsea neighbourhood is very much at the centre of the independent gallery movement of the city. Knowing which galleries to visit can be overwhelming, but for visiting art lovers there is a Thursday night Chelsea art crawl every week. The galleries are free to enter, and many of them serve up free wine as well. Art, wine, and money in your wallet – what could be better?

(http://chelseagallerynights.herokuapp.com)

84. Chow Down at Queens Night Market

Since New York City has four very defined seasons with very cold winters, street food isn't something you'll find in the winter months (aside from questionable street hot dogs), but a totally different world of street food can be found during the summer, and one of our favourite spots to fill our stomachs is the Queens Night Market, open from April til October. Queens is one of the most ethnically diverse parts of the United States, and this market reflects that. Will you go for Malaysian laksa, Chinese bao buns, Mexican tostadas, Israeli falafel, or something altogether different?

(Corona Park, Queens; http://queensnightmarket.com)

85. Hit a Few Balls at Dyker Beach Golf Course

If your idea of the perfect getaway involves spending plenty of time on the golf course, you're in luck because NYC has no shortage of courses that cater to the middle classes who work hard in the week and like to relax on the green on the weekends. There are quite a few courses to choose from, and Dyker Beach Golf Course is one of the best. The golf course dates back to 1895, which makes it one of the oldest in the States.

(1030 86th St & 7th Ave, Brooklyn; www.dykerbeachgc.com)

86. Drink Beers and Eat Wings at Blind Tiger

NYC is a city full of incredible attractions, but sometimes it's the simplest things in life that make us the happiest, isn't it? Well, if your legs are hurting from all the museums and sightseeing, why not take things easy for a hot second and treat yourself to some beer and wings? If that sounds good to you, Blind Tiger, an ale house in Manhattan is the place to be. Their list of draught and bottled beers is second to none, and their chicken wings with Korean BBQ sauce never fail to hit the spot.

(281 Bleecker Street; www.blindtigeralehouse.com)

87. Watch the Skateboarders in Tribeca Skatepark

In many ways, New York City is a youth city that embraces all the subcultures of teenagers, and a good way of embracing the city's youth culture is by seeking out one of New York's skate parks. There's actually quite a number of these, and the Tribeca Skatepark is perhaps the most famous. This park is right on the waterfront, which makes it a lovely place to hang out on a sunny day, and we think that you'll be amazed by the talents of the young locals who hang out and skate there.

(N More Street; www.hudsonriverpark.org/explore-the-park/activities/tribeca-skatepark)

88. Sip on Wines at the Brooklyn Uncorked Festival

When you think of wine country in the United States, your thoughts will probably wander to California and the Napa Valley. Of course, that's a great place for any wine lover to visit, but believe it or not, there's also some wonderful wines being produced in New York state, and you can try some of them for yourself at the annual Brooklyn Uncorked Festival, which is committed to shining a light on New York wineries. The festival takes place at the end of May each year.

89. Take in the Views From the Loopy Doopy Rooftop Bar

As soon as we heard of the name of the Loopy Doopy Rooftop Bar, we knew that it was a place where we would want to hang out, pretty much all the time. And when we actually visited, we would confirm that we were not wrong. This is actually the rooftop bar of the fancy Conrad Hotel in Manhattan. It has a stunning view over New York Harbour, great cocktails, and there are even boozy ice pops that will get you tipsy in the cutest way.

(Conrad New York, 102 North End Ave; www.conradnewyork.com/dine/loopy-doopy-rooftop-bar)

90. Start Your Day With a Coffee From Sweetleaf

New York is a city full of coffee lovers, so if you need to start your day with a strong hit of caffeine before you can do anything, you are in luck. But with so many incredible coffeehouses dotted around the city, how do you know which is the best for easing into your day of exploration? There are lots of gooduns but take it from us that Sweetleaf, which has locations in Queens and Brooklyn, is one of the best. It's the best espresso we've had in the city. *(10-93 Jackson Ave, Queens; http://sweetleafcoffee.com)*

91. Stroll Through Socrates Sculpture Park

With space at a premium in New York City, it's amazing how some discarded places have been reinvented to create real value. Socrates Sculpture Park is one such place. Built on the site of a former landfill site, the park is now home to large scale sculptures and multimedia installations – a wonderful blending of nature and culture. It also

hosts many free community events such as yoga, capoeira, and outdoor film screenings.
(32-01 Vernon Blvd, Long Island City; http://socratessculpturepark.org)

92. Get a Sugar Rush at Chinatown Ice Cream Factory

New York is nothing short of swelteringly hot in the summer months, and while you could escape the heat by having a lie down in your air conditioned room, we think that slurping on some ice cream is a much better method. And when we're in the mood for some ice cream deliciousness we always head straight to the Chinatown Ice Cream Factory. As this ice cream joint is located in Chinatown, it's the Asian flavours that steal the show. The lychee flavour is consistently a bestseller, while the durian is something daring for foodie adventurers.
(65 Bayard St, Chinatown; www.chinatownicecreamfactory.com)

93. Catch a Drag Show at Boots & Saddle

New York is one of the most gay friendly cities in the whole world, and even if you aren't gay yourself, it can be a wonderful idea to hit up a few of the gay bars, drink, and make some new friends. One of the gay bars that we return to time and again is called Boots & Saddle, located in the super gay Greenwich Village area. The reason we love it so much is simple – the drag shows! The entertainers are polished, hilarious, irreverent, and super talented. *(100A 7th Ave S; www.bootsandsaddlenyc.com)*

94. Keep Kids Entertained at the New York Hall of Science

Travelling with kids is no easy thing. They require constant attention and entertainment, and although NYC is an entertainment city, it's also a very grownup city with grownup things for grownup people. But somewhere that kids are sure to love is the New York Hall of Science, even if science isn't their best subject at school. Located in the heart of Queens, virtually everything in this museum is interactive with a Science Playground and Design Lab where young people can get to grips with design and engineering in a fun way.

(47-01 111th St, Corona; http://nysci.org)

95. Find the Treasures of the City's Trash

A city as large and iconic as New York city is always going to be brimming full of hidden treasures, and one of the best places to discover these in NYC is at the Treasures in the Trash Collection, a garbage depot that showcases weird and wonderful items that have been salvaged from the trash. Inside you'll find an astonishing collection of items, with everything from vintage furniture to typewriters, a plaque from the original World Trade Center to discarded Christmas decorations.

96. Eat Lots of Dim Sum at Jim Fong

Dim Sum is the traditional Chinese breakfast of Chinese people, consisting of lots of little dumplings and other bites. We think that it's one of the most deliciously decadent ways to start the day, but you don't have to fly to China to get your hands on the good stuff. In fact, there is awesome dim sum to be found all over New York, and Jim Fong is our favourite of these eateries. The dining hall is almost intimidatingly large, but that means you'll always get a table. Don't leave before trying the deep fried bacon wrapped shrimp.

(20 Elizabeth Street; http://jingfongny.com)

97. Find Your Super Power at Brooklyn Superhero Supply

Are you a total geek at heart? Don't worry, you can be open with us, and when we're in New York we love to embrace our inner geek as well, and the place to do just that is at Brooklyn Superhero Supply. This store is pretty much what it says on the tin; inside you will find everything you could possibly desire to indulge your most private superhero fantasies with costumes for every superhero and supervillain that you can possibly think of.

(372 5th Ave, Brooklyn; www.superherosupplies.com)

98. Walk Brooklyn Bridge at Sunrise

New York is, without a doubt, a city of bridges, and perhaps the most iconic of all these bridges is Brooklyn Bridge, connecting Brooklyn to Manhattan. Completed in 1883, it has a total span of 486 metres and it is the first steel-wire suspension bridge in world history. A huge number of vehicles traverse the bridge each day, but it's also open to pedestrians, and there is no better time to walk the bridge than at sunrise. You'll witness a gorgeous sky, the skyline coming into view, and you can take pictures without hordes of people around you.
(www.nyc.gov/html/dot/html/infrastructure/brooklyn-bridge.shtml)

99. Take in a Performance From the New York Philharmonic

If you are a classical music fan, it almost goes without saying that catching a performance by the

New York Philharmonic Orchestra while you're in the city would be a very good idea indeed. This orchestra dates all the way back 1842, which makes it one of the oldest and most renowned musical institutions in the country, and they have already played more than 14,000 concerts. Their home is the Geffen Hall in the Lincoln Center for the Performing Arts, so be sure to keep up with their programme of events.

(https://nyphil.org)

100. Treat Yourself to Doughnuts From Doughnut Plant

If you're on a diet, New York City might not be the best destination for you, but if you can put the calorie counting aside for a hot moment, you'll have a hell of a lot of fun filling up your stomach, and one of our favourite treats in the city are the doughnuts from Doughnut Plant. There are so many flavours that you can try something new every time you come back. If you're on a romantic trip,

the rose petal doughnuts hit the spot, and if you want comfort food, we love the pumpkin doughnut.
(379 Grand Street; http://doughnutplant.com)

101. Dance Til You Drop at Bembe

It's because of places like Bembe that New York has earned its reputation as a haven for party lovers, and it's always on our radar for a fun night of Friday night dancing. We really like this Williamsburg dancing spot because it's not as full on as a major club, but it still has incredible DJ talent, great drinks, and enough space to dance. If you want to meet some locals and simply have a great night that you may or may not remember the next day, get yourself to Bembe.

(81 S 6th St, Brooklyn; www.bembe.us)

Before You Go…

Thanks for reading **101 Coolest Things to Do in New York City.** We hope that it makes your trip a memorable one!

Keep your eyes peeled on www.101coolestthings.com, and have a wonderful time on the East Coast.

Team 101 Coolest Things